Timmy

Make Pineapple Tarts

LEVEL 2

by Ruth Wan-Lau
Illustrated by Eliz Ong

Published by Little Knights
An imprint of Armour Publishing
Block 1003 Bukit Merah Central #02-07 Singapore 159836
Email : sales@armourpublishing.com
enquiries@armourpublishing.com
Website: www.armourpublishing.com

19 18 17 16 15
6 5 4 3 2

Printed in Singapore

ISBN 978-981-4597-72-2

National Library Board, Singapore Cataloguing-in-Publication Data

Wan-Lau, Ruth, 1976-
Timmy & Tammy make pineapple tarts / by Ruth Wan-Lau ; illustrated by Eliz Ong. – Singapore : Little Knights, [2015]
pages cm. – (Let me read. Level 2)
ISBN : 978-981-4597-72-2

1. Pastry – Juvenile fiction. 2. Baking – Juvenile fiction. I. Ong, Eliz. II. Title. III. Series: Let me read. Level 2.

PZ7
428.6 -- dc23 OCN894025566

Chinese New Year is coming soon. Grandma is making pineapple tarts today.

"Can you smell something nice?"

Timmy says.

Grandma is cooking the pineapple.

It has become pineapple jam!

"This is going to be delicious!"

Tammy says.

"What is the next step, Grandma?"
Tammy says.
"Do what I do," Grandma says.
Timmy and Tammy follow Grandma.

Mix
Mix
Mix

Grandma mixes the dough.

Tammy mixes her dough.

Timmy mixes his dough.

Grandma rolls the dough into a ball.

Tammy rolls her dough into a ball.

Timmy rolls his dough into a ball.

Flat

Grandma makes the dough flat.

Tammy makes her dough flat.

Timmy makes his dough flat.

"Time to bake the tarts!"
Grandma says.
"Will you two help me to
wash up, please?"
"We will!"
Timmy and Tammy say.

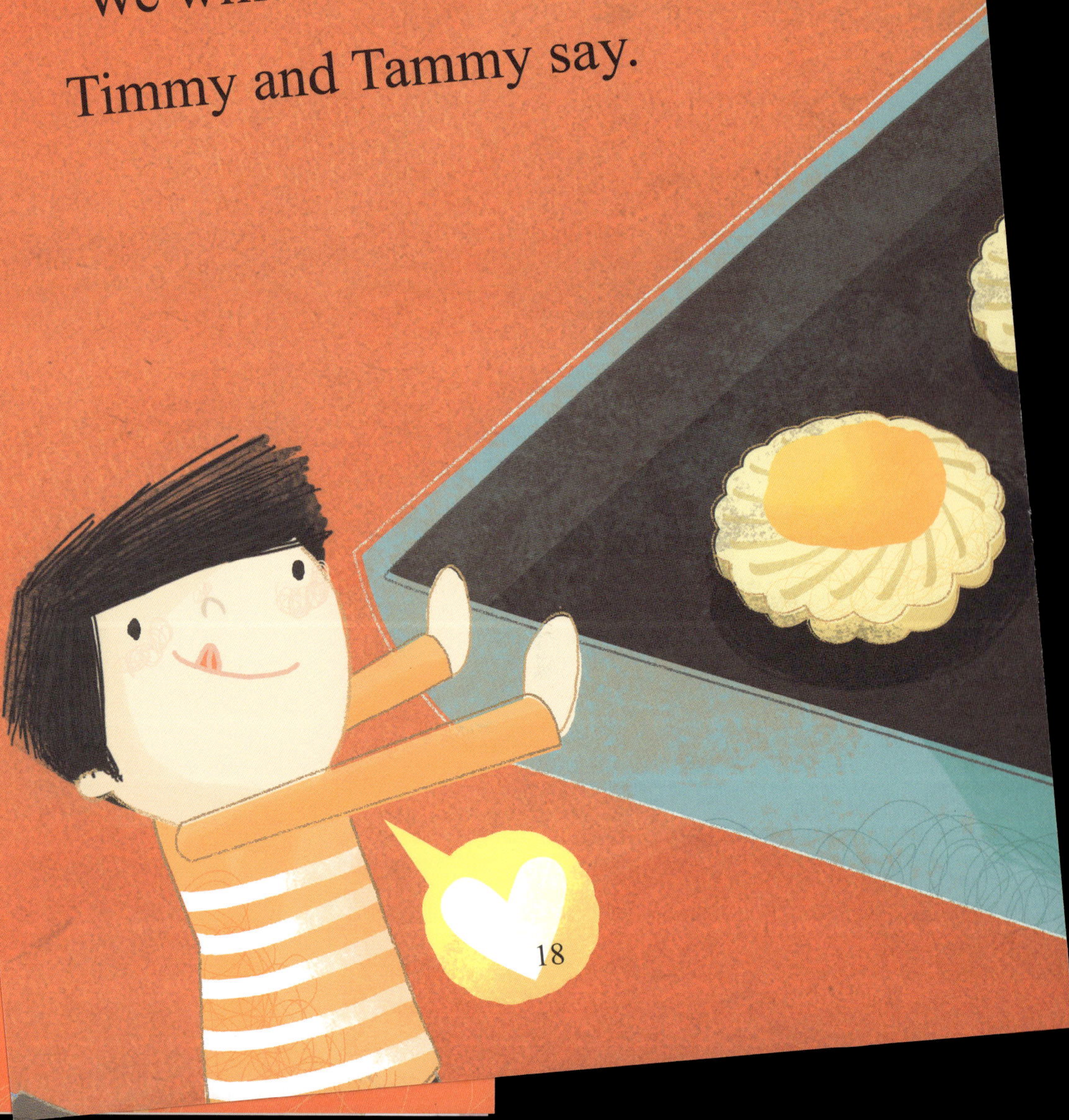

Grandma tells us a funny joke
as we wash the dishes.
Timmy shares a funny joke too.
Then, it is Tammy's turn.
Everyone laughs.

The pineapple tarts are ready!

"You two can be the first to try them," Grandma says.

They taste super good!

Happy Chinese New Year, everyone!

Look at the pictures from the story and say the order they should be in.

More in the *Let Me Read* series

Level 1

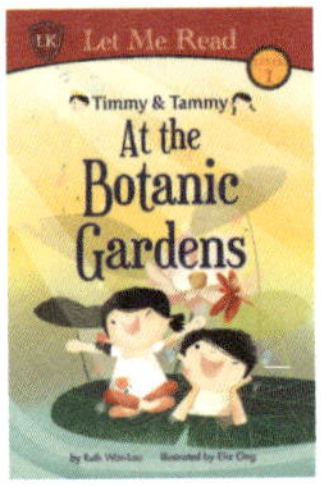

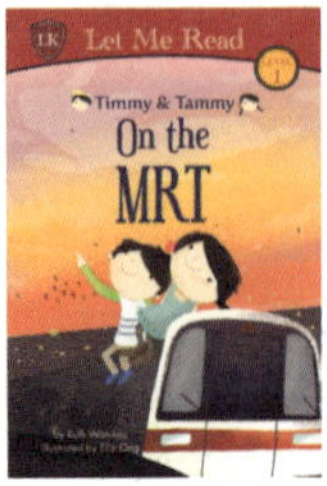

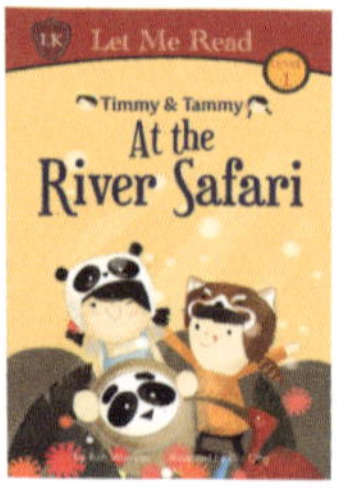

Level 2

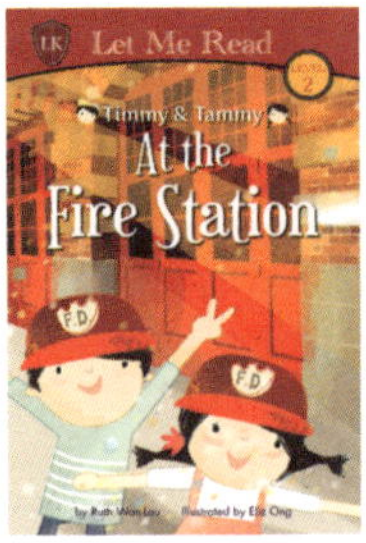

Level 3

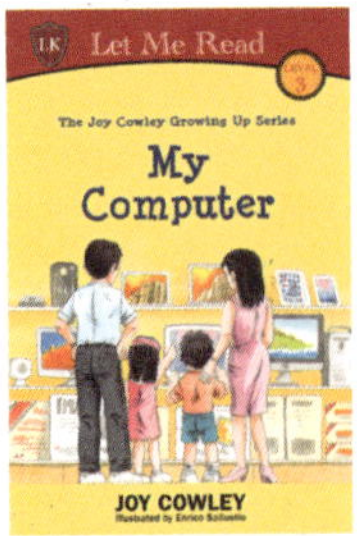

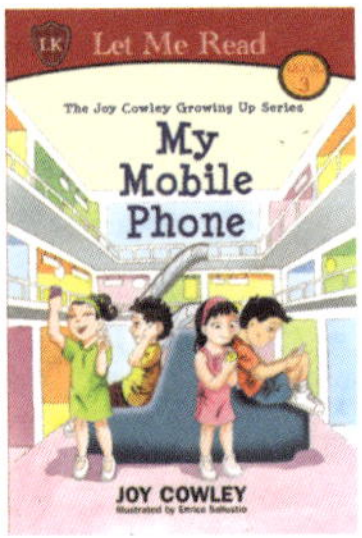

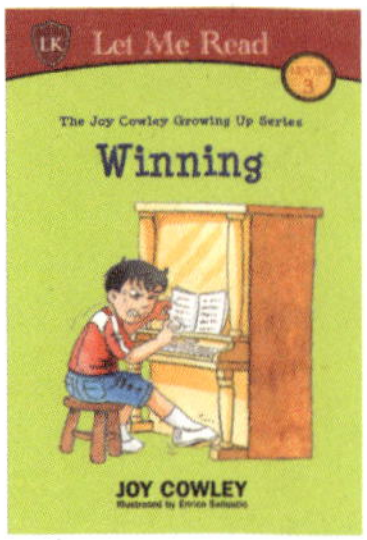

Genius Level 4

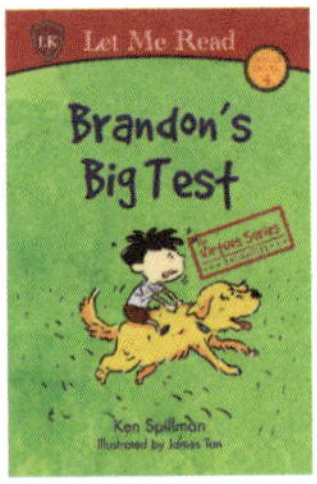

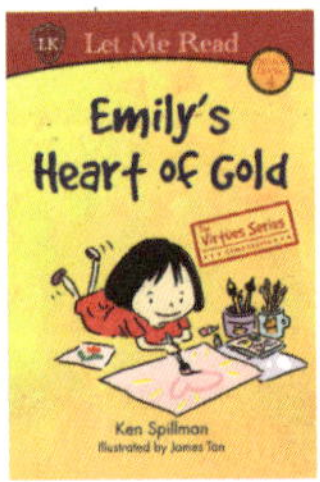

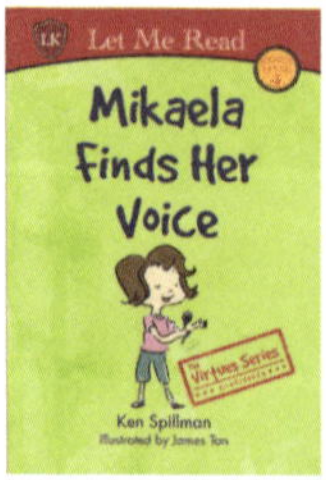